Elizabeth Miles

Heinemann Library
Chicago, Illinois

Designed by David Oakley at Arnos Design
Originated by Ambassador Litho Ltd
Printed in Hong Kong

07 06 05 04 03
10 9 8 7 6 5 4 3 2 1

Library of Congress Cataloging-in-Publication Data
Miles, Elizabeth, 1960-
   Mouths & teeth / Elizabeth Miles.
      p. cm. -- (Animal parts)
Summary: Briefly describes how animals of the land, sea, and air use
their different kinds of mouths and teeth for eating, drinking, and
other purposes.
   ISBN 1-40340-018-0 (HC), 1-40340-427-5 (Pbk)
   1. Mouth--Juvenile literature. 2. Teeth--Juvenile literature. [1.Mouth. 2. Teeth.]
I. Title: Mouths and teeth. II. Series: Miles, Elizabeth, 1960- . Animal parts.
   QL857 .M56 2002
   591.4--dc21
                              2001006755

Acknowledgments
The author and publishers are grateful to the following for permission to reproduce copyright material: p. 4, Corbis Stock
Market/Charles Gupton; p. 5, BBC NHU/Bruce Davidson; pp. 6, 30, Digital Stock; p. 7, BBC NHU/Colin Seddon; pp. 8, 25, BBC
NHU/Lynn M. Stone; p. 9, 27, Corbis; p. 10, Corbis/George D. Lepp; p. 11, NHPA/A.N.T.; p. 12, SPL/Tom McHugh; p. 13, OSF/Don
Skillman; p. 14, NHPA/Image Quest 3-D; p. 15, NHPA/Stephen Dalton; p. 16, NHPA/N. A. Callow; p. 17, BBC NHU/Martin Dohrn;
p. 18, OSF/Satoshi Kuribayashi; p. 19, Bruce Coleman Collection/Antonio Manzanares; p. 20, NHPA/Andy Rouse; p. 21, NHPA/Jane
Knight; p. 22, BBC NHU/David Kjaer; p. 23, Bruce Coleman Collection/Chris Gomersall; p. 24, OSF/Tom Ulrich; p. 26, NHPA/David E.
Myers; p. 28, Bruce Coleman Collection/Hans Reinhard; p. 29, BBC NHU/Richard Du Toit.

Cover photograph reproduced with permission of Oxford Scientific Films.

Every effort has been made to contact copyright holders of any material reproduced in this book. Any omissions will be rectified in
subsequent printings if notice is given to the publisher.

Some words are shown in bold, **like this.** You can find
out what they mean by looking in the glossary.

Contents

Mouths for Eating

Every animal has a mouth. Some, like people, have teeth. You use your mouth to eat and drink. You must eat and drink to stay healthy and grow.

This gorilla is using its teeth to bite and
chew its food. The teeth and mouths of
different animals are shaped differently.

Jaws, Lips, and Tongues

Many animal mouths have a top and a bottom part. These are called jaws. Teeth grow down from the top jaw and up from the bottom jaw. Crocodiles have strong jaws for catching **prey.**

Dogs and many other animals have soft lips around their mouths. Their lips and tongues move easily and help them to eat and drink.

Flat Teeth

Animals have different types of teeth for eating different kinds of food. Some animals, such as cows, have flat teeth for grinding and chewing plants.

Sheep are plant-eaters too. They often
graze on grass. They use their flat teeth
to grind the grass into small bits.

Pointed Teeth

Animals that eat meat have sharp, pointed teeth. Lions use their four longest teeth to stab and hold their **prey.** They eat animals such as zebras and antelopes.

Many meat-eaters that live in the ocean have razor-sharp teeth. The gray nurse shark uses its teeth to catch and eat food.

Teeth for Cutting and Chewing

Some rats eat both meat and plants. They bite into wooden food crates and use their teeth to cut and chew the packages inside.

Bears have teeth for eating meat and plants. They use their pointed teeth for catching and eating fish. They use their flat teeth to grind up fruits and berries.

Toothless Mouths

Many animals do not have teeth. They use other mouthparts to bite and chew. A tortoise has a strong, sharp **beak.** It can bite through fruit, grass, and leaves.

Locusts and other **insects** have sharp,
strong jaws for cutting and chewing plants.
A **swarm** of millions of locusts can eat a
whole **crop** within a few hours.

Sucking Mouths

Many flies have long mouthparts. A fly dribbles **saliva** onto its food to turn it into a liquid. Then it sucks the liquid up through its long, tube-shaped mouth.

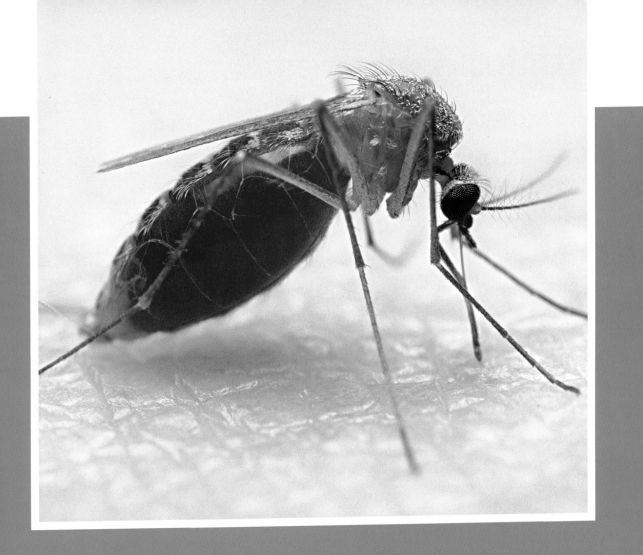

Some mosquitoes feed on blood. They have needle-sharp tubes that pierce a hole in the skin of a person or animal. Then they suck some blood up through the tube.

Sticky Tongues

A toad's tongue is at the front of its mouth. The toad can flick its tongue out very far to catch **insects.** The tongue is sticky, so the insect cannot get away.

A giant anteater's tongue can be twice as
long as your arm. It pushes its long nose
into an ants' nest. Then it flicks out its sticky
tongue to lick up the ants.

Wide Tongues, Rough Tongues

Animals with a long, wide tongue use it for drinking. A tiger uses its tongue to **lap** up water. The tongue also helps the tiger taste what it eats and drinks.

Many **mammals** use their tongues to lick themselves clean. A cat has a long, rough tongue. It spends a lot of time licking its fur.

Beaks

Birds have no lips or teeth. Instead, they have **beaks.** A woodpecker has a sharp, narrow beak. It drills holes into tree bark with its beak to find **insects** to eat.

Bald eagles are birds of **prey.** They catch
small animals such as fish, birds, rabbits, and
squirrels to eat. Their strong, hooked beaks
tear the meat from the bones.

Beaks for Eating Fish

Herons have long, sharp **beaks.** They stand in shallow water looking for fish or frogs to eat. When the heron sees one, it spears the fish or frog with its beak.

Pelicans have huge beaks with a **pouch** of skin underneath. To catch fish, they scoop up a mouthful of water. They let the water drain out, then swallow any fish left behind.

Mouths in the Ocean

Some whales have **baleen** instead of teeth. Baleen is like a **sieve,** or strainer. A whale takes a mouthful of water. Then it squeezes the water out, trapping tiny sea creatures in its mouth to eat.

A moray eel lives in shallow water. It hides in between rocks, waiting for **prey** to pass by. It uses its mouth of sharp teeth to catch fish, octopuses, or crabs.

Mouths for Carrying

Besides eating, drinking, and catching food, some animals use their mouths in other ways. A bird often carries food in its **beak** to feed its chicks.

Lions' mouths are strong enough to kill other large **mammals.** They can also be used gently. If a lioness senses danger, she uses her mouth to carry her **cubs** to safety.

Fact File

- Some sharks have rows of teeth. When one row wears out, a new row moves forward.

- Vipers are snakes with a dangerous bite. They have very sharp teeth called fangs. Poison passes through the fangs into the snake's **prey.**

- The roughness of an animal's tongue helps it to lick dirt from its fur and **lap** up more water when it is drinking.

Hippopotamuses have strong jaws and teeth.

Glossary

baleen   tiny hard sieve in some whales' mouths

beak   mouth with a hard edge and no teeth (sometimes called a bill)

crop   fields of fruit, vegetables, or cereals

cub   young animal, such as a cheetah or a lion

graze   eat low-growing grass or plants

insect   small animal with three main parts to its body and six legs

lap   use the tongue to drink

mammal   animal that feeds its babies with the mother's milk. People are mammals.

pouch   pocket made of skin

prey   animals hunted as food

saliva   juices in mouths that make food soft and wet

sieve   tool that traps small objects, but lets liquid flow through

swarm   large numbers of insects flying together

More Books to Read

Miles, Elizabeth. *Ears*. Chicago: Heinemann Library, 2003.

Miles, Elizabeth. *Eyes*. Chicago: Heinemann Library, 2003.

Miles, Elizabeth. *Noses*. Chicago: Heinemann Library, 2003.

Miles, Elizabeth. *Paws and Claws*. Chicago: Heinemann Library, 2003.

Index

DISCARD